Loving and Living the Mass

SECOND EDITION

FR. THOMAS KOCIK

ZACCHEUS PRESS
Bethesda

Nihil Obstat:	Rev. Mark Knestout
	Censor Deputatus
Imprimatur:	Most Reverend Barry C. Knestout
	Auxiliary Bishop of Washington
	Archdiocese of Washington
	August 18, 2011

The *nihil obstat* and *imprimatur* are official declarations that a book or pamphlet is free of doctrinal or moral error. There is no implication that those who have granted the *nihil obstat* and the *imprimatur* agree with the content, opinions or statements expressed therein.

Library of Congress Cataloging-in-Publication Data

Kocik, Thomas M.
 Loving and living the Mass / Thomas Kocik. -- 2nd ed.
     p. cm.
 Includes bibliographical references.
 ISBN 978-0-9830297-3-1 (alk. paper)
 1. Mass. I. Title.
 BX2230.3.K63 2011
 264'.36--dc23
                                                              2011034589

10 9 8 7 6 5 4 3 2 1

To learn more, please visit our webpage:

www.zaccheuspress.com

Pater Misericordiae, emitte Spiritum Tuum ut omnium hunc
librum legentium et mentum illuminet et cor tangat.
Sit instrumentum ad exaedificandum Regnum Tuum.
Per Christum Dominum nostrum. Amen.

To my parents,

Thomas and Dorothy,

my first teachers

in the central lesson

of the Holy Mass:

sacrificial love

CONTENTS

Preface to the Second Edition

This book originated as a weekly series in *The Anchor*, the official newspaper of the Diocese of Fall River, Massachusetts. I thank Father Roger J. Landry, the executive editor, for inviting me to contribute the series and for encouraging me to have it published in a single volume. I am likewise grateful to Zaccheus Press for publishing my work.

Inserting into the original work my reference for every statement concerning the prayers, ceremonies, and theology of the Mass would encumber the text and unduly distract the non-specialist for whom it was written. Therefore, to maintain the original's informality and broad appeal, I have added footnotes sparingly. In the same vein, I have given the English titles of the few patristic writings cited, even when the secondary source bears the Latin title. The Bibliography lists the chief sources used in writing this book as well as other works for those readers interested in further study.

The official Latin text of the Mass is contained in a book known as the *Missale Romanum* (Roman Missal). In 1970, a few years after the close of the Second Vatican Council, Pope Paul VI published a new edition of the Roman Missal in Latin. Some parts of the new Missal appeared in English straightaway, although the first official English translation in its entirety dates to 1973. In 2010, the Holy See approved the final portions of a revised English translation of the Missal of Paul VI in its most recent edition, the one published in 2002. This second edition of *Loving and Living the Mass*, revised in the light of the new English translation, includes a new chapter explaining why and how the new translation came about, as well as a new chapter on the importance of ritual in human life and divine worship.

The Order of Mass described herein conforms to the third edition of the Roman Missal (2002). Excerpts from the revised English translation are as found in *The Roman Missal, Third Edition* (United States Conference of Catholic Bishops, 2010), prepared by the International Commission on English in the Liturgy (ICEL). Biblical quotations are from the Revised Standard Version (RSV) – Catholic Edition.

T. K.
Fall River, Mass.

PART ONE

Preliminaries

Introduction

Do you enjoy going to Mass? (Be honest.) You may be a very good Catholic and still feel that Mass attendance is something of a chore having little to do with "real life." Many Catholics go to Mass every Sunday or Saturday evening because it would be a serious offense against God not to, or because they have become so used to going every week that it has become mechanical. These reasons are good enough as far as they go, since the primary purpose of the Mass is not to please us but to worship our Creator. Still, if your fidelity to Sunday Mass rests on nothing more solid, your attitude at Mass is likely to be nothing more than penitential obedience. If you really understand what is happening at Mass and how the Mass should impact your life, you'll find Mass anything but boring. This book is meant to help you deepen your appreciation of the Catholic Church's supreme act of worship, and to live the meaning of the Mass in your daily life. We will "walk through" the Mass from its beginning to end, exploring the significance of its various prayers, symbols and gestures. Before we begin our tour of the Mass, however, some background information will be helpful.

Let's start with the word "Mass." In the early centuries of Christianity the Mass was known by other names, such as the "Breaking of Bread," the "Eucharist," and the "Lord's Supper." The name "Mass" was not used until many years later (and only in the Western or Latin Church) when the custom began for the deacon to dismiss the people formally from the service. "Go, it is the dismissal," he said. The phrase in Latin is "Ite, missa est."[1] And *missa*, "dismissal," is in English "Mass." Eastern Christians, both Orthodox and Catholic, refer to the Mass as the "Divine Liturgy." Whatever the name used, the Mass is the Church's obedient response to Jesus' command at the Last Supper: "Do this in remembrance of me" (Lk 22:19).

What, in fact, we are doing—and what, if anything, Christ is doing in our doing of it—will be explained in the next chapter. Then we will look at a broad outline of the Mass and what happens in each section. As further preparation for our tour, we will survey the inside of a typical Roman Catholic church and note

---

[1] The Latin phrase is idiomatic and so admits of multiple translations, for example, "Go, it has been sent" and "Go, it is ended" ("it" being the Church or congregation).

the sacred vessels, vestments, and other items used to celebrate the Eucharist. The preliminaries conclude with an explanation of both the "body language" of the Mass, meaning the postures and gestures Catholics use in worshiping God, and the necessity of formal ceremonial. By then, we should be well prepared to begin our tour.

Don't worry about remembering everything. After all, the apostles didn't fully understand all that was happening at the Last Supper. They were told only that the bread which Jesus broke was no longer bread but His actual Body, and that the wine in the cup was no longer wine but His Blood. Accepting this mystery of faith, the apostles understood enough to make them active participants in our Lord's act. They were sharing in what was, with the crucifixion that was to take place the next day, the first Mass. So you don't have to be a theologian to "get something" out of the Mass, or to put your best into it. Of course, the more you know about the Mass, the better you can appreciate its indispensable role in your spiritual life. A wise monk once remarked that for a Catholic to become holy without the Mass would be as impossible as for a Catholic who loved the Mass not to become holy. Before you turn the page, think that one out.

What Is the Mass?

"Do this in remembrance of me," Jesus told His disciples at the Last Supper (Lk 22:19). And Christians have obeyed that command for two thousand years. What, in fact, are we doing? And what, if anything, is our Lord doing in our doing of it?

The first three Gospels tell us the Last Supper was a Jewish Passover meal, a memorial of God's rescue of the Israelites from Egyptian slavery (as recounted in the Book of Exodus). The Jews believed that their annual Passover feast not only commemorated God's saving action in the past, but also made that salvation present again to those who ate this meal. At the Last Supper, Jesus changed the meaning of the Passover. From then on, it would be praise and thanksgiving (Eucharist derives from the Greek word for "thanksgiving") in memory of His death and Resurrection, which frees us from sin and death. He identified the bread and wine used at the meal with His Body and Blood. To make the Eucharist a memorial of His death and Resurrection, Jesus ordered His apostles to remember Him by taking bread and wine and declaring over them, in Jesus' name, that they are His Body and Blood, sacrificed on the Cross and raised to new life. By eating and drinking His Body and Blood in faith, Christians share in God's holiness, power, and life. Even more, this sacrificial banquet is a foretaste of the marriage supper of the Lamb and His Bride the Church (Rev 19:9).

Because Holy Thursday and Good Friday are intimately related, the Eucharist is both the Lord's Supper *and* the sacrifice of His Body and Blood. When the priest repeats Jesus' words spoken at the Last Supper, "This is my Body... This is my Blood," bread and wine become in very truth the Lord's Flesh and Blood. Then, with hands uplifted in adoration, thanksgiving, praise and supplication, we offer to God, through the hands of the priest and together with him, the same self-offering which Jesus inaugurated at the Last Supper and completed on the Cross for the salvation of the world. Since Christ rose from the dead and is now in heaven, we must exclude any thought of His physical death being present in some mysterious way each time His sacrifice is offered on our altars. The Mass is not a repetition of the sacrifice on Calvary, nor is it a mere commemoration of that sacrifice. Rather, Christ's once-for-all sacrifice is made present at Mass sacramentally under forms of bread and wine. Nothing more perfect can go up to God from this earth than the sacrifice of Christ, and nothing more perfect can come down to us from heaven than what that sacrifice has merited for us: eternal life in God.

So the Mass is much more than an elaborate ceremony for producing Christ's sacramental Body and Blood. In the Mass we unite ourselves with the crucified and risen Savior in the very act by which He redeemed the world. By receiving Holy Communion, we proclaim our will to be one with Christ's sacrifice, for Communion is the *fruit* of His saving death and Resurrection. The main idea is to have the mind of Christ in us (Phil 2:5), to get so near to Him in spirit that we pray what He prays, do what He does, and love as He loves. Our will to be one with Christ, giving ourselves to God our Father through, with and in Christ's own self-giving—this is really the whole point about going to Mass. And God, who is never outdone in generosity, in turn gives us grace upon grace.

Outline of the Mass

Picture the Mass as a well designed structure, with major sections into which all the prayers, readings, psalms, and gestures fit in correct balance. If we try this, we find that the Mass has two major parts: the service of the Word of God, and the Eucharistic sacrifice celebrated, by divine institution, in the form of a holy meal. The first major part is called the Liturgy of the Word and is preceded by Introductory Rites; the second is called the Liturgy of the Eucharist and is followed by the Concluding Rites. Part Two of this book contains a step-by-step explanation of the Mass. We'll consider the meaning of the various prayers and actions, not all of which are of equal importance. For now, let's view the Mass in the broadest outline.

Introductory Rites. Mass begins with a processional song or psalm verses to greet Christ in the person of the priest. After the entrance song (said or sung), the priest greets the people. Then priest and people make a public confession of sinfulness followed by a prayer for pardon. On Sundays and feast days, the Christian hymn of praise known as the *Gloria* is then sung or said. Finally, the priest prays a prayer of petition called the *Collect*.

Liturgy of the Word. This section is simple in its structure, but of deepest importance. On Sundays and solemn feasts, there are three readings taken from Sacred Scripture. During most of the year, the first is taken from the Old Testament and the second from one of the New Testament letters; the third is always taken from one of the four Gospels. On weekdays there are usually two readings: the first is taken from the Old Testament or a New Testament letter, the second from the Gospels. A Responsorial Psalm based on God's own inspired hymnal, the Book of Psalms, is sung or recited after the first reading. The Scripture readings and psalms are God's message of love to us, His adopted children, made capable of calling Him Father by our baptism. Together with the homily, these readings represent God's teaching through the Church, the call and invitation of the Lord so that all may gather at the altar of thanksgiving and sacrifice. On Sundays and solemnities, after the homily, we recite the Nicene Creed, a profession of orthodox Christian faith dating to the fourth century. Finally, we entrust the needs of the Church and the whole world to God in the Prayer of the Faithful or General Intercessions.

Liturgy of the Eucharist. This part of Mass is more complex, but it can be summed up briefly. After a brief preparation of bread and wine for the sacrifice, there are two great subdivisions: first, the Eucharistic Prayer (or Canon) itself; then the holy banquet of Communion. Christ the Lord, through the ministry of the ordained priest and the power of the Holy Spirit, changes bread and wine into His own Body and Blood, which He offers to the Father in atonement for our sins (as He did on Calvary), and then gives Himself to us as imperishable Bread for our pilgrimage. We pray silently, thanking God and asking for all that this Sacrament promises. The priest unites our prayers in the Prayer after Communion.

Concluding Rites. The Mass ends quickly with a blessing and a dismissal. We who have been fed by God's Word in Scripture and by the Word-made-flesh in the Eucharist are sent forth to live the deepest meaning of the Mass, Christ's sacrificial love, in all the circumstances of our daily life.

A Look Inside the Church

Now let's have a look at the inside of a typical Roman Catholic church, since that is where the Roman rite of Mass is ordinarily celebrated.[2] At the entrance is a basin of holy water. On entering church, a Catholic dips his right hand in the holy water and makes the Sign of the Cross on himself. The water is a reminder of baptism, the sacrament that made us members of Christ's mystical Body the Church.

From wherever we stand in the larger center section of the church, called the *nave*, our attention is

[2] The Catholic Church is a splendidly diverse family of Churches in communion with the Bishop of Rome (the Pope) and, on that basis, with one another. Each Church has its own liturgical, theological, spiritual, and disciplinary patrimony which, taken as a whole, is called a "rite." The Western or Latin Church, comprising the vast majority of Catholics, follows the Roman Rite, whereas the Eastern Churches (most of which have Orthodox counterparts) follow five other principal rites: the Alexandrian, the Antiochene or West Syrian, the Armenian, the Byzantine, and the Chaldean or East Syrian.

drawn to the *sanctuary* (from the Latin *sanctus*, "holy"), which is raised a few steps above the nave to emphasize its importance. (In some churches, the sanctuary is divided from the rest of the interior by a low gate or altar rail a few feet tall.) In the center of the sanctuary is the *altar*, preferably made of a single natural stone to remind us of the rock of sacrifice in the Old Testament (Gen 22:1-9; cf. Ex 20:25; Deut 27:5; Josh 8:30-31) and to represent Christ, the Rock of salvation (1 Cor 10:4). The altar is both the table of the Lord's Supper and the place where the sacrifice of Calvary is made present. Within it are sealed relics of martyrs, linking us to the earliest days of Christianity when Mass was offered on the tombs of those valiant believers who continued the Passion and death of Jesus in their own lives.

Behind or near the altar is the *tabernacle*, often plated with gold or silver and lined with silk, in which are kept the consecrated breads, or *Hosts*, reserved for Communion to the sick and for adoration by the faithful. The Catholic Church teaches that once the bread and wine are consecrated at Mass, they cease to be bread and wine and become instead the Body and Blood of Christ, whose Real Presence in the consecrated elements remains as long as the appearances of bread and wine last. (The consecrated bread and wine are also called the Blessed Sacrament.) A *sanctuary lamp* burns near the tabernacle night and day to indicate Christ's sacramental Presence, which makes the church literally the house of God. For this reason, Catholics maintain a reverent silence in church, not talking except when necessary, and genuflecting on entering and leaving church or passing before the tabernacle.

When Mass is celebrated, at least two lighted *candles* are on or near the altar (four or six for more solemn Masses). To remind us that the Mass is the sacrifice of Calvary made present sacramentally, a *crucifix* (not a bare cross or an image of the risen Lord) is on or near the altar. Also in the sanctuary (behind or to the side of the altar) is a *chair*, slightly elevated, where the priest as presiding celebrant sits during parts of the Mass, as well as a *lectern* or *ambo* from which the Word of God is announced. There may also be a *cantor's stand* opposite the ambo, for the use of the cantor who guides the congregation in singing.

In addition to these, there are other things inside the church that are important but neither directly involved with, nor absolutely required for, Mass: images of the Blessed Virgin Mary, the saints and angels; the confessional booths and/or reconciliation rooms; the stations of the cross; the baptismal font and Paschal candle; and perhaps other altars or shrines. Whether or not Mass is being celebrated, the whole church should be arranged so as to invite prayer and contemplation, expressing visibly the sense of heaven on earth.

The Tools of the "Trade": Sacred Vessels and Other Items

Without being flippant, we may call the sacred vessels and other objects used at Mass the tools of the trade—if by "trade" is meant not a profession but an exchange. You see, the Mass is a holy exchange in which we give ourselves to God in union with Christ's sacrifice, and God in turn gives us Christ's very Body and Blood as food for our earthly pilgrimage. In this chapter, we'll note the items used for this marvelous exchange of gifts we call the Mass.

The *paten* is the plate on which the priest's Host rests. Imagine yourself on the paten with the bread, offering to God your mind and heart, your soul and body, all that you have and are.

The *chalice* is the cup containing the wine that becomes the Precious Blood of Christ; it should be made of precious metal or at least noble material that does not easily break or rust. Pour out your heart into the chalice with the wine, and put into it all your hopes and fears, joys and sorrows, love and adoration, your whole self.

The *ciborium* (from the Latin *cibus*, "food") is another vessel of precious metal; it holds the altar breads to be consecrated and distributed for the Communion of the faithful.

The *Roman Missal* is the book the priest uses for the prayers of the Mass. Many of these prayers date back to the early centuries of the Church. Even if these prayers do not express how you feel at a given moment, you should still pray them in a spirit of communion with your brothers and sisters in Christ.

The *Lectionary* is the book containing all the Scripture readings and is used at the lectern or ambo. A separate *Book of the Gospels* may be used by the deacon for proclaiming the Gospel readings. Faith comes through hearing God's inspired word (Rom 10:17).

The *altar cloth* is the white covering used for the tabletop (*mensa* in Latin) of the altar; it symbolizes Christ's burial shroud. The lighted *candles* on or near the altar represent Christ, the Light of the world (Jn 8:12). The *crucifix* on or near the altar reminds us that the sacrifice of Calvary is sacramentally renewed in the Mass.

Other noteworthy items are: the *chalice veil* (optional), either white or the color of the Mass vestments, used to cover the chalice before the Preparation of the Gifts and again after Communion; the *burse* (optional), a square, envelope-like container for holding the corporal; the *pall* (optional), a cardboard square covered with linen used to cover the mouth of the chalice, particularly to keep out insects and dust; the *corporal* (from the Latin *corpus*, "body"), a square of linen folded into nine parts on which rest the paten and chalice during the Liturgy of the Eucharist; the *cruets* containing the water and wine; the *purificator*, a cloth used to dry the chalice after its cleansing; and the *finger towel* used to dry the priest's hands after they are washed at the Preparation of the Gifts.

Also used on occasion are the *thurible*, a metal bowl, hanging by one or three chains, which holds charcoal and incense; and the *aspergillum* (from the Latin for "sprinkle"), a container for the holy water used to sprinkle the congregation as a reminder of baptism.

We, like the sacred vessels, were made to receive Christ. Saint Thérèse of Lisieux wrote in her autobiography that the Lord "does not come down from heaven every day to lie in a golden ciborium: He comes to find another heaven which is infinitely dearer to Him—the heaven of our souls, created in His image, the living temples of the adorable Trinity!"[3]

---

[3] Thérèse of Lisieux, *The Story of a Soul*, trans. John Beevers (Garden City, N.Y.: Image Books, 1957), p. 66.

Dressing Accordingly: Sacred Vestments

In design, the vestments normally worn at Mass are similar to the clothes worn in the Greco-Roman world at the time of Christ. They mark how old the Catholic Church is. Over the centuries, they acquired symbolic meanings. Each vestment has a relation to Christ, and each bears a message for us.

The first item the priest puts on is the *amice*, symbolizing the "helmet of salvation" (Eph 6:17). Once a cowl worn to keep the ears of monks warm in icy monastery chapels, it is now a white rectangular garment placed over the shoulders and tucked in at the neck; it need not be worn if the *alb* completely covers the neck. The alb (from the Latin for "white") is a linen garment reaching to the ankles; it symbolizes purity and recalls the baptismal garment worn when the new Christian "put on Christ" (Gal 3:27).

The *cincture*, a sign of chastity, is a cord used to tie the alb snug at the waist; it need not be used if the alb already fits well.

The *stole* is a scarf-like vestment worn over the alb and under the chasuble or dalmatic (see below). The priest wears his stole around his neck so that it hangs equally down in front; the deacon wears his stole over the left shoulder and tied at his right side. The stole symbolizes the clerical state and suggests the obedience and fidelity with which the priest or deacon should perform his sacred duties.

The *chasuble* (from the Latin for "little house") is an ornate poncho-like garment covering all other vestments; it symbolizes the supreme virtue of charity, in which all Christians are to abound.

The *dalmatic* is the deacon's garment, comparable to the chasuble but with open sleeves and square-cut at the bottom; it symbolizes service.

Lastly, the *mitre* is the tall, two-pointed hat worn by the bishop, symbolizing the union of the Old and New Testaments. Bishops may also wear the dalmatic under the chasuble.

Except for the alb, vestment colors vary. *White*, symbolizing joy and purity, is used during the Christmas and Easter Seasons and on all feast days of Christ, Our Lady, and saints who are not martyrs. For particularly solemn celebrations, *gold* may be substituted.

Red is worn on Palm Sunday, Good Friday, Pentecost, and at Masses in honor of the Holy Spirit and martyrs; it represents blood as well as the Holy Spirit who descended in the form of fiery tongues (Acts 2:2-3).

Violet (purple), a penitential color, is used during Advent and Lent. *Rose* may replace violet on the Third Sunday of Advent (Gaudete Sunday) and the Fourth Sunday in Lent (Laetare Sunday) as a call to rejoice in the approaching feasts of Christmas and Easter. (*Gaudete* and *laetare* are Latin words for "rejoice.")

Black, the color of mourning, may be worn at the Mass of Christian Burial and at other Masses for the dead (such as All Souls' Day). *Violet* may be used instead of black. *White* is likewise a legitimate option in the United States and certain other countries.

Green, the color of new life, is used during so-called Ordinary Time.

Mass vestments are worn not only by the celebrant but also by concelebrating priests. If a priest is present but not functioning as a concelebrant, he wears the *cassock* and *surplice* rather than Mass vestments and dons the stole when receiving and/or administering Communion. The cassock, a full-length smock, is black for priests, purple for bishops and higher-ranking monsignors, red for cardinals, and white for the Pope; the surplice is a white, knee-length vestment worn over the cassock.

Vestments cloak the priest's own personality, helping us to focus instead on the true Priest, Christ, who speaks and acts through the ordained priest. They also symbolize humility, purity, contrition, and other dispositions we need in order to put our soul, mind, and body into what Christ is doing at Mass, and to be good Christians when we leave church.

The "Body Language" of the Mass: Postures and Gestures

The Church assigns certain postures and gestures throughout the Mass in order to engage the whole person, body and soul, in worshiping almighty God.

Standing is the position of reverent attention and is especially appropriate for the Gospel and Creed. It is also the ancient posture for prayers of petition, and so we stand for the principal prayers of petition, namely, the Collect, the Prayer of the Faithful, the Prayer over the Offerings, and the Prayer after Communion.

Sitting indicates attentive listening, which is particularly appropriate during the Scripture readings (prior to the Gospel) and the homily.

Kneeling signifies humility and adoration. Except for the celebrant and concelebrants (if any are present), all kneel during the consecration of the bread and wine, when Christ becomes sacramentally present on the altar. In the United States, the congregation kneels for most of the Eucharistic Prayer.

Genuflection is the bending of the right knee in adoration. The priest genuflects after consecrating the bread and again after consecrating the wine, before receiving Communion, and when approaching and leaving the tabernacle. Whether or not Mass is taking place, we should genuflect whenever we pass before the tabernacle or the altar (if the Blessed Sacrament is present on the altar), to acknowledge Christ present in the most holy sacrament of the Eucharist.

Bowing may be either profound (bending at the waist) or simple (bowing of the head). Whether during or outside Mass, a profound bow is made to the altar (which symbolizes Christ)—unless the Blessed Sacrament is present on it or is reserved in the tabernacle behind it, in which case a genuflection is made. A profound bow is likewise made when reciting the article of the Nicene Creed regarding the Incarnation ("and by the Holy Spirit was incarnate of the Virgin Mary, and became man"). The priest bows his head when speaking the holy Names of Jesus and Mary as well as the name of the saint of the day.

Raising of the hands is the ancient priestly gesture of supplication in the Jewish tradition. For this reason, the priest raises his hands at different points throughout the Mass, especially during the Eucharistic Prayer and the Lord's Prayer.

Striking one's breast is a sign of humility and sorrow for sin and is used during the *Confiteor* ("I confess…") of the Penitential Act (see p. 35).

Making the *Sign of the Cross* reminds us of the price of our salvation. Mass begins and ends with the Sign of the Cross. The priest blesses the gifts of bread and wine by making the Sign of the Cross over them before they become the Body and Blood of the Lord; he also blesses the incense with the Sign of the Cross before using it.

There is always a temptation to minimize the importance of bodily postures and gestures, on the assumption that the more plain and informal our worship is, the more "spiritual" and "sincere." It is good to ponder what Blessed John Henry Newman, the great Anglican convert (and later Cardinal) of the nineteenth century, said of this mindset concerning the worship of the One who created all things visible and invisible, bodies as well as souls: "Our tongues must preach Him, and our voices sing of Him, and our knees adore Him, and our hands supplicate Him, and our heads bow before Him, and our countenances beam of Him, and our gait herald Him."[4] Holy vestments and vessels, noble furnishings, forms of prayer, orders of ministers, ceremonies of devotion: all these, Newman said, signify the coming into this world of Christ's invisible Kingdom. With this wisdom in mind, we are well prepared to begin our tour of the Mass.

---

[4] J.H. Newman, "The Visible Temple," *Parochial and Plain Sermons* (San Francisco: Ignatius Press, 1997), p. 1365.

Why *Ritual* Worship?

Rituals, it seems, serve a very human need. They preserve traditions and bridge transitions, renewing individuals and communities alike. Rites of passage mark our movements from youth to adulthood, from school to full-time employment, from single life to vowed commitment, from work to retirement, from life to death to what lies beyond. Birthdays, anniversaries, holidays, and festivals punctuate each passing year. By nature repetitious and thus predictable, rituals are to everyday life what good punctuation is to grammar: they make distinctions and clarify meaning. Something as simple as a family sitting down to dinner at an appointed time is a ritual. As the family separates "dinner time" from the rest of the day, the shared meal receives privileged attention and becomes extraordinary (literally, outside the ordinary).

The Mass, too, is a ritual. Its prescribed words,

ceremonies, and actions are meant to lift the worshiper out of the ordinary and into the realm of the sacred. Gestures such as the elevations of the Host and chalice, the reverent kisses of the altar, incensations, genuflections, and profound bows convey the sense of God's presence more powerfully than spoken words. These are not mere decorations, but the means by which the Church's faith is exhibited, transmitted, and interiorized. In word and action, the Mass presents us with the mysteries that have been delivered to us by the "Holy Spirit sent from heaven, things into which angels long to look" (1 Pet 1:12).

In particular, the Mass makes present, in a sacramental way, our Savior's lifelong sacrifice and love, the last and most dramatic expression of which was His death on Calvary. When Christ "incorporated," that is, when He formed a body for Himself from the Christian people, He made it possible for the faithful of all times and places to step into another world, another life: His own priestly life of perfect worship and unwavering love of the Father. Christ's love of God is really what saved us, for it motivated and gave saving force to His human life and achievements. In the sacrifice of the Mass, we compress into sixty or thirty minutes what was the substance of thirty years of worship in spirit and in truth: Christ's daily thoughts and words, His patient labors and healing gestures and, finally, His Passion and death. Nowhere on earth are we closer to our salvation than we are when worshiping God at Mass in and through the risen Lord.

In everyday life as in religion, ceremony confers significance upon an event. The more important the event, the more formal the ceremony. The graduation exercises for a kindergarten class, while festive, will lack the pomp of a high school commencement, and both of these will pale in comparison to graduation ceremonies at West Point or Annapolis. The dignity and reverence which clothe—or, at any rate, ought to clothe—our Eucharistic celebrations befit the profoundly sacred nature of the Mass as Christ's sacrifice and ours, a holy communion with the Lord and a foretaste of the heavenly banquet.

There is no evidence to suggest that people today need ritual less than earlier generations. Even so, one sometimes hears the objection that the Mass would be more interesting and more "relevant" if, instead of following the same pattern and employing many of the same prayers day after day, week after week, it allowed for greater variation and creativity. Fixed ceremony and prepackaged recitations weigh down the soul and stifle the Spirit—or so the argument goes.

Such thinking contains a grain of truth: the Church's prayer should always have a point of contact with individual experience, lest it become sterile. What is missed, however, is the distinction between personal prayer and *liturgical* prayer. The liturgy is, by definition, the official public worship of the Church, Head and members.[5] Our disposition when praying as members of the Church gathered for worship is, or at any rate ought to be, different from when we pray as individuals. Liturgical celebrations, Eucharistic or otherwise, require a specific order of procedure, which enables the assembly to worship as one community.

If the liturgy is not a private devotion at which other people happen to be present, neither is it primarily a gathering of the faithful expressing their identity as a community in Christ. That is a secondary aspect of the liturgy, not its nature. The liturgy is God's saving action in our midst, made present through the hierarchical observance of rites and the offering of prayers handed on in Tradition from apostolic times and developed in the Church throughout her long history. Through word and sacrament, God gives Himself to us in Jesus Christ, the Eternal Priest. Faith and love move us to respond as best we can to render this sacred encounter worthy of the presence of God, of the infinite merits of Christ, of the sacrifice of the martyrs,

[5] (As defined in Pope Pius XII's 1947 encyclical *Mediator Dei*.) Immediately, the Mass comes to mind, and rightly so, for at the high point of the liturgy, as at the center of Christian living, stands the Eucharist. However, the liturgy encompasses the whole spectrum of rites contained in the Church's official liturgical books: the sacraments, the myriad blessings of persons and objects, Viaticum and the pastoral care of the sick, the rites of Christian burial, the different hours of prayer in the Divine Office that sanctify the entire day, and so on.

of the hopes of all the redeemed. Toward this end, we use all manner of our gifts: words, gestures, vestments, art, architecture, and music, both vocal and (in the West) instrumental. These gifts themselves take on a sacred character. There is, of course, always the latent danger of grasping the shadow for the substance, the earthly symbol for the heavenly reality. Sometimes this danger emerges as a kind of "ceremonialism," a clinging to external forms that have outlived their meaning and purpose. But vigilance to avoid this danger must not prevent us from recognizing that the liturgy, as the chief embodiment of the truths that come down from Christ and the apostles, should convey a sense of the objective, the unchanging, and the universal.

So where does that leave creativity and personal preferences? In addition to liturgical prayer, the Church's tradition includes a wealth of other prayer forms, both personal and communal: the various methods of private prayer and such devotional practices as the rosary, novenas, the stations of the cross, *lectio divina* (the slow, contemplative praying of the Bible), and visits to the Blessed Sacrament. Prayer meetings, visits to local shrines, and family devotions are occasions for spontaneous acts of faith, hope, and love.

A final point needs to be made in this connection. As critics of art and literature know, creativity even in the secular sphere is enhanced, not diminished, by fidelity to traditions handed down from the past. For the believing Catholic who is heartily disposed to enter into Christ's love for His Father but also His love for mankind, the familiar flow of the Mass does not stifle personal faith; it nurtures it, sometimes by just keeping the embers warm, and other times by setting the flames roaring.

Saint Benedict, the father of Western monasticism, taught his monks in chapter 19 of his Rule to pray the psalms "in such a way that our minds may be in harmony with our voices."[6] That same idea is conveyed in the story of a woman who complained to her rabbi after a synagogue service, "The service does not say what I mean"; to which the rabbi replied, "Madam, your job and mine is to mean what the service says." With the grace of God in your mind and heart, the prayer of the whole Church can become your own prayer, drawing you ever more deeply into the saving life of Christ in all its vigor and fullness.

[6] *RB 1980: The Rule of St. Benedict in English*, ed. and trans. Timothy Fry, O.S.B. (Collegeville, Minn.: The Liturgical Press, 1981), p. 47.

PART TWO

A Tour of the Mass

The Introductory Rites

The Sign of the Cross and Greeting

Now we begin our walk through the Mass. We learned that the essence of the Mass is sacrifice: first Christ's, then ours. So, it is fitting that the Holy Sacrifice begins with the Sign of the Cross. But before we ponder the rich meaning of that ancient gesture (which may date to the time of the apostles), let's take note of what happens just prior to signing ourselves with the cross.

An opening hymn accompanies the procession of the priest and other liturgical ministers to the sanctuary. This hymn, or entrance antiphon (usually a verse or two from the Psalms), sets the mood for the day's celebration. The procession reminds us that we are a "pilgrim" Church, on the way to eternity. Upon reaching the sanctuary, the priest and ministers genuflect to the Blessed Sacrament, if the tabernacle is in the sanctuary; otherwise, they bow to the altar, which symbolizes Christ. The priest kisses the altar, in effect greeting Christ. (If a deacon assists, he too kisses the altar.) On solemn occasions, the priest then incenses the altar; the rising smoke signifies our prayers ascending to heaven (Ps 141:1-2). The priest and people then make the Sign of the Cross, after which the priest wishes for the people God's grace and peace. This greeting is more than a simple courtesy; it is a prayer for the salvation of all present, which is why secular greetings such as "Good morning!" are inappropriate.

What does the Sign of the Cross mean? In a word: love. It was for love of sinners that Christ died and rose. The Cross is the emblem of His redeeming and victorious sacrifice, the triumph of God's love over the powers of evil. By making the Sign of the Cross, we show our acceptance of the salvation won for us on Calvary. No need, then, to brood over our sins and failings; rather, resolve to love God more firmly through deeper intimacy with the risen Lord. The Sign of the Cross also expresses our willingness to take up our cross daily and follow Christ (Lk 9:23). We bear our cross when, for example, we keep the Commandments in spite of ridicule or difficulty, or when we put up with inconveniences for the sake of others.

Not only does God love us, but God *is* love (1 Jn 4:8, 16). We make the Sign of the Cross "in the Name of the Father, and of the Son, and of the Holy Spirit." God is not a solitary being living in isolation, but an eternal community of three persons. His very essence is a loving union: the Father loves the Son, the Son loves the Father, and this mutual love is the Holy Spirit. Because we humans are created in the image of the Trinity, we too are relational beings, needing to love and to be loved. God calls us to eternal life, which is a sharing in the life and love of the Trinity (Jn 17:21). Without grace, however, we cannot have eternal life, which is why we should pray, go to church, and receive the sacraments regularly. But we must also observe the Commandments, since love of God and love of neighbor are inseparable. As the three divine persons dwell in one another, so we must "dwell" in others, living in and for them (see Jn 17:21-22).

You probably won't remember all this every time you bless yourself with the Sign of the Cross. Just let that simple gesture remind you that the Christian life is more akin to self-sacrifice than to self-improvement. By crucifying our self-indulgence, by "dying" to ourselves, we "walk in newness of life" (Rom 6:4) as children of the Father, whose Spirit makes us brothers and sisters of His only-begotten Son and of one another.

The Penitential Act

After the Sign of the Cross and greeting comes the Penitential Act. The Bible always urges repentance as a prelude to worship. We therefore acknowledge our unworthiness to approach the all-holy God, while at the same time placing our trust in His boundless mercy.

The priest invites us to examine our conscience by calling to mind our sins. Recalling our sins is hard to do without pausing for a moment. We need a period of silence to remember—and repent of—the bad things we did and the good things we neglected to do. I remember celebrating Mass and hearing, after only five seconds of silence, a woman in the front pew whisper impatiently, "What's he waiting for?" Maybe she was hard of hearing and didn't hear me say, "Let us call to mind our sins." Or perhaps she was one of the many who, having been schooled in the gospel of self-acceptance, cannot think of anything to be sorry about. The sense of sin, the sense that there is another order of authority by which we are judged—these haven't been totally lost, but they have been eroded. And that's a dangerous thing. The Gospels tell us that physical and emotional health is not the be-all and end-all of existence. As Jesus might say today, it is better to enter heaven with a guilt complex than to enter Gehenna brimming with self-righteousness.

After a moment of silence, the priest and people together pray the *Confiteor*: "I confess to almighty God...." As a gesture of humility, we strike our breast at the words, "through my fault, through my fault, through my most grievous fault." Notice that we speak in the first person "I" rather than as part of a "we." How appropriate, since sin builds barriers not only between the individual and God but also between the individual and other people. For good reason, then, we ask the loving intercession of the whole Communion of Saints which is the Church: "I ask blessed Mary ever-Virgin, all the Angels and Saints, and you, my brothers and sisters, to pray for me to the Lord our God."

The priest then prays for the pardon of his own sins and the sins of all present: "May almighty God have mercy on us...." However, this prayer of absolution does not substitute for the sacrament of penance, which in most circumstances is necessary for the forgiveness of mortal sins.

The Penitential Act concludes with a humble and hopeful prayer called the *Kyrie eleison*, Greek for "Lord, have mercy." Together with the accompanying invocation *Christe eleison* (Christ, have mercy), these are the only Greek phrases now found in the Roman rite of Mass.

Instead of the *Confiteor* followed by the absolution and *Kyrie*, two other forms of the Penitential Act are allowed. One consists of two brief invocations said by the priest (or a deacon or another minister), each followed by the people's response:

Priest: Have mercy on us, O Lord.
People: For we have sinned against you.
Priest: Show us, O Lord, your mercy.
People: And grant us your salvation.

The other consists of three invocations said by the priest, deacon, or other suitable minister, to which the people respond *Kyrie eleison* after the first and third invocation and *Christe eleison* after the second. For example:

Priest: You were sent to heal the contrite of heart: Lord, have mercy.
People: Lord, have mercy.
Priest: You came to call sinners: Christ, have mercy.
People: Christ, have mercy.
Priest: You are seated at the right hand of the Father to intercede for us: Lord, have mercy.
People: Lord, have mercy.

The *Kyrie* follows, unless it has already been used in one of the forms of the Penitential Act.

On Sundays, the Penitential Act may be replaced with the Rite of Blessing and Sprinkling of Holy Water. This recalls our baptism, when we died with Christ and rose with Him to the new life of grace. All the sacraments receive their power from the Passion of Christ; the blood and water that flowed from His pierced side on the Cross symbolize the Church's two chief sacraments, baptism and the Eucharist. Christ's sacrifice is the source of all grace and holiness, and nothing in the Mass is unrelated to it.

It has been said that we Christians are an "Alleluia people," because at the heart of our faith is Easter and we know our story will end in resurrection. That's true, provided we live according to the law of love in obedience to the Lord. Yet how often we prefer our will to His! This is why, before we sing "Alleluia," we cry out, "Lord, have mercy."

The *Gloria* and Collect

On Sundays outside Advent or Lent and on solemnities and feasts, after the Penitential Act comes the *Gloria*, a hymn of praise that begins with the words sung by angels to herald the newborn Savior's birth: "Glory to God in the highest, and on earth peace to people of good will" (Lk 2:14).[7] Also known as the Angelic Hymn and the Greater Doxology (*doxa* in Greek means glory or praise), the Gloria was introduced in the Mass of Christmas Day by Pope Saint Telesphorus in the second century. Later, its use was extended to other days, but only at Masses celebrated by a bishop. It was not used as it is now until around the ninth century. All four motives of prayer are found in the Gloria: adoration ("We praise you, we bless you, we adore you, we glorify you"), thanksgiving ("we give you thanks..."), petition ("... receive

---

[7] RSV: "... and on earth peace to men of good will."

our prayer"), and contrition ("... have mercy on us").

It is said that the bad angels rebelled against God and were cast into hell because they could not tolerate the thought of the Incarnation. As the more intelligent creatures, they were far superior to feeble-minded human beings. But the Incarnation would make human beings superior to the angels within the heavenly hierarchy. Indeed, as God willed it, the Father's only Son assumed our sin-scarred humanity and so, in this sense, became lower than the angels. At the end of time, the saints—human men and women—will be resurrected and placed beside Jesus and Mary, the King and Queen of heaven and earth. The good angels have the humility to grasp this truth in joy. How fitting that we sing the Angelic Hymn as we prepare to receive the Lord here on earth once again, this time in sacramental form, but in a presence no less real than what Our Lady, Saint Joseph and the shepherds beheld that first Christmas night, when heaven rejoiced and hell fumed.

The Introductory Rites of the Mass conclude with the Collect prayer, so called because its purpose is to gather or "collect" the prayers and aspirations of the congregation. Like the entrance antiphon, the Collect varies and sets the tone for the day's Mass. The priest invites the congregation to pray. Then, after a brief silence, he sings or says the Collect while standing with arms and hands extended. (Pictures in the Roman catacombs depict the early Christians praying thus.) The Collect consists of an invocation ordinarily addressed to God the Father, a brief petition asking for what is essential in our Christian life, and a conclusion referring to Christ, our Mediator with the Father (1 Tim 2:5; cf. Jn 14:6). We make the Collect our own prayer and assent to it by responding "Amen" (Hebrew for "So be it!").

Up to this point, the prayers of the Mass have led us in a kind of crescendo, starting with a public acknowledgment of our sins before God and preparing us to hear the good news of salvation and to participate in the offering of Christ's sacrifice. Glory to God and peace to those who are united with Him by grace. That is precisely what the Mass does: In word and sacrament, we glorify God in union with His angels and saints, into whose heavenly company we will enter provided we leave this life in Christ's friendship.

THE LITURGY OF THE WORD

The Scripture Readings

After the Collect prayer, the mood of the Mass changes. We have been speaking to God in prayer; now, in the Liturgy of the Word, God will speak to us through His inspired prophets, apostles, and evangelists. Instruction, given in the biblical readings and homily, is an essential part of our preparation for the Eucharistic sacrifice.

The Scripture readings are taken from the *Lectionary*, a liturgical book containing the Mass readings for each day of the year. The Sunday Lectionary follows a three-year cycle (designated Cycles A, B and C) of three readings. The First Reading usually comes from the Bible of the Jews, the Old Testament, and relates to the Gospel passage, showing how God prepared His chosen people, Israel, for the coming of Jesus the Messiah. (The word "Gospel" derives from

41

the Old English word for "good news," meaning the good news of God's saving work for us in Christ.) The Second Reading is usually taken from an epistle of Saint Paul or another apostle. The Gospel readings are arranged so that, for most of the year, Cycle A relies on Matthew's Gospel, Cycle B on Mark's, and Cycle C on Luke's. John's Gospel is used in all three cycles and especially Cycle A on the Sundays in Lent. The weekday readings follow a two-year cycle (designated Year I and Year II), which includes many Bible passages not covered on Sundays.

Now let's consider the order of the Liturgy of the Word. A lay reader or officially installed lector goes to the ambo and reads the First Reading as we sit and listen attentively. Next comes the Responsorial Psalm, sung or recited in alternation between the reader (or cantor) and the congregation. This psalm, taken from God's inspired hymnal, the Book of Psalms, is meant to be a meditative response to the message of the First Reading. On Sundays and solemnities, the Responsorial Psalm is followed by the Second Reading.

After a period of silent reflection, the cantor intones the Alleluia, a joyful cry of praise (from the Hebrew *hallelujah* for "Praise God"). So connected to an attitude of rejoicing is the Alleluia that it is replaced during Lent by another acclamation. At this time, we stand in reverent anticipation of the Gospel proclamation. Christ is about to speak in a unique way to us, His Church. A special *Book of the Gospels* may be used instead of the Lectionary, and on solemn occasions the sacred text is incensed as the reader is flanked by two acolytes with lighted candles. Only an ordained minister (ideally a deacon) may read or sing the Gospel at Mass. If he is a deacon, he first seeks the celebrant's blessing; if a priest or bishop, he prepares himself by bowing before the altar and praying in a low voice: "Cleanse my heart and my lips, almighty God, that I may worthily proclaim your holy Gospel."

Once at the ambo, the minister greets the congregation with "The Lord be with you." He then introduces the passage while making a small cross with his thumb on the page, then on his forehead, lips and chest. We likewise sign ourselves with the cross. This ritual action signifies our desire to open our minds and hearts to the good news of the Gospel and to share that good news with others. The reading concludes with the formula "The Gospel of the Lord" and we respond, "Praise to you, Lord Jesus Christ." The minister then kisses the sacred book (just like the altar, since both are points of contact with the Lord) while praying inaudibly, "Through the words of the Gospel may our sins be wiped away." (In Masses celebrated by a bishop, the deacon or priest carries the Book of the Gospels to the bishop to be kissed, whereupon the bishop may impart a blessing to the people with the sacred book.) By our response of faith to Christ, we enter into the blessings promised by the Good News. To help us live out that response, God further instructs us through the preaching of His ordained ministers.

The Homily

One of the oldest elements of the Mass is the homily, an informal instruction on the spiritual life. Unlike a sermon, which is a talk on any religious topic, a homily draws its inspiration from the liturgical texts and especially from the Scripture readings. Long before Christ's time, commentary on the Scriptures was part of the Sabbath liturgy in the synagogue. We know too that Saint Paul preached at the Eucharist (Acts 20:7, 11). And Saint Justin Martyr, a second-century Church Father, reports in his description of the Mass that once the reader has finished, "the President warns and exhorts us in a speech to follow these glorious examples."[8]

---

[8] Justin, *First Apology* 67, 4; quoted in Adrian Fortescue, *The Mass: A Study of the Roman Liturgy* (London: Longmans, Green & Co., 1912; repr. Albany, N.Y.: Preserving Christian Publications, 1999), p. 284. By "President" is meant the one who presides over the Eucharistic service, normally the bishop in the early Church.

Now, as then, the purpose of the homily is to help us gain more insight into God's Word and to live in accordance with the Faith we profess. On Sundays and holy days a homily is mandatory; it is recommended on other days and especially during Advent and Lent. Usually the homily relates to the Gospel passage just proclaimed. Yet the other readings also provide a very rich mine, and the preacher who consistently ignores them leaves that mine untapped.

In the Scriptures, God speaks to us through one of His inspired messengers or, as in the case of the Gospel, through His own divine Son. In the homily, God speaks through His ordained servant. By Church law, the homilist at Mass must be a bishop, priest, or deacon; moreover, only with the bishop's permission may a priest or deacon preach. This is not primarily because of the theological training needed to preach sound doctrine. After all, many laypersons and Religious are well educated and more eloquent than their clergy. Rather, it is because the sacrament of holy orders — the fullness of which is the office of bishop — confers a unique grace enabling the minister to teach, sanctify, and shepherd the faithful in a supernatural way, as Christ's instrument.[9]

"Do you understand what you are reading?" Saint Philip asked the Ethiopian eunuch who was reading the prophet Isaiah; and the eunuch replied, "How can I, unless someone guides me?" (Acts 8:30-31). When

[9] *Catechism of the Catholic Church*, no. 1585.

we Catholics read and hear Scripture, we accept the guidance of our Church, whose God-given teaching authority (Mt 28:18-20; Mk 16:15) is vested in the apostles and their legitimate successors, the Pope and the bishops united with him (Mt 16:19). The Holy Spirit guides the Church "into all the truth" (Jn 16:13) and preserves her from teaching false doctrine. Long before the New Testament was completed, the Church was preaching and teaching God's Word and celebrating the Eucharist. The Church decided which writings were to be included in the Bible. She shielded the Bible from barbarian attacks and copied it in her monasteries centuries before the printing press. As "the pillar and bulwark of the truth" (1 Tim 3:15), she infallibly interprets God's revelation (cf. 2 Pet 1:20-21; 3:15-16). The Bible, then, is the Church's book, a fruit of her living Tradition of contemplation, preaching, teaching, and worship. Those who think Scripture is sufficient as a guide to faith and life should take to heart Saint Augustine's famous remark: "But I would not believe in the Gospel, had not the authority of the Catholic Church already moved me."[10]

A brief period of silence should follow the homily, to allow time to meditate on the biblical and preached Word. Then ask our Lord to help you be like Zaccheus in Luke's Gospel, firmly resolving to put into practice the saving message you have just received.

---

[10] Augustine, *Against the Letter of Mani* 5, 6; quoted in the *Catechism of the Catholic Church*, no. 119.

The Profession of Faith (Creed)

Christians are expected to know and make known the answer to Jesus' question, "Who do you say that I am?" (Lk 9:20). From earliest times, Christians have had a summary of faith, or creed (from the Latin *credo*, "I believe"), spoken over them, or by them, at their baptism. When belief in Christ's divinity was under attack, the bishops of the Catholic Church gathered at Nicea (in modern-day Turkey) in the year 325 and declared that if Jesus was not God, He was neither worthy to be worshipped nor capable of redeeming the world. Using one of the baptismal creeds in common use, the Council of Nicea added language that would express correct belief about God's Son. The result was the core of what we call the Nicene Creed: "I believe in one Lord Jesus Christ, the Only Begotten Son of God, born of the Father before all ages. God from God, Light from Light, true God from true God, begotten, not made, consubstantial[11] with the Father..." We can say Christ is God because He is the second person of the divine Trinity, the eternal Son who became flesh and blood in the womb of the Virgin Mary (Jn 1:1-18).

Catholic, Orthodox, and many Protestant Christians recite or sing (or, at any rate, hear) the Nicene Creed every Sunday. Unfortunately, many Christians fail to see the relevance of a written and spoken creed to their life of faith. "Jesus didn't hand on a creed," they object; "He taught the love of God and neighbor." They fail to realize that for Christianity, as for Judaism and Islam, belief in the one true God who revealed himself in persons and events requires some kind of formula for confessing the faith. Already in the Old Testament there are confessions, most notably the *Shema*: "Hear, O Israel: The Lord our God is one Lord" (Deut 6:4). And in the New Testament, Saint Paul, drawing on the *Shema*, used the formula: "There is one God, the Father, from whom are all things and for whom we exist, and one Lord, Jesus Christ, through whom are all things and through whom we exist" (1 Cor 8:6). It is a small

---

[11] The terms "substance," "essence," and "nature" in classical Western philosophy denote *what* someone or something is: a tree, a cat, a human being, etc. To confess the Son as "consubstantial" with the Father is to say that the Father and the Son have the same nature (in this case, Godhood or Divinity) and therefore the Son is God no less than the Father. By virtue of the Incarnation, Jesus Christ is both fully God and fully man in one divine person, namely, God the Son.

step from the language of the Bible to the words of the Apostles' Creed, "I believe in God the Father almighty," or the opening line of the Nicene Creed, "I believe in one God, the Father almighty, maker of heaven and earth...."

The Nicene Creed is part of the great Tradition of orthodox Christian belief. "Tradition" comes from the Latin noun *traditio*, something handed over. Christ's saving message is preserved, transmitted, and lived in the Church's Tradition, a many-splendored thing encompassing Scripture, the ancient creeds, the decrees of the Popes and ecumenical councils, the writings of the Church Fathers, the sacred liturgy, and the ministry of shepherds guided by the Holy Spirit in interpreting the truths of revelation. In a word, Tradition is the total life of Christ's Body, the Church, through time. How fitting, therefore, that the Liturgy of the Word should include the Creed. For God's written Word is not understood apart from the historic faith and life of the Church. By the same token, Tradition is not another source of God's Word alongside the Bible, but must always be shaped by Scripture.

"Deeds, not creeds!" may be a catchy slogan for those who think religion is a matter of the heart and not the head. But love without truth is mere sentimentality and ultimately deceitful and even destructive (see 2 Pet 2:1). Christianity is believing and living "in spirit and *truth*" (Jn 4:24). And how we are to love (deeds) cannot be sustained apart from an answer to the question why (creeds).

The Prayer of the Faithful

In the first few centuries of the Church, those preparing for baptism ("catechumens") and penitents were dismissed from Mass immediately after the homily. Only baptized Catholics who could receive Holy Communion were permitted to stay for the remainder of the Mass, known as the "Mass of the Faithful" and now termed the Liturgy of the Eucharist. Once the catechumens and others had departed, the faithful offered prayers for the Church and her ministers, for the state, for travelers, for their enemies, for the poor—in short, for all classes of people. When the practice of dismissing catechumens and others ceased around the sixth century, the Prayer of the Faithful fell out of use in the Roman-rite Mass.

The liturgical reform following the Second Vatican Council (1962-65) reintroduced both the Prayer of the Faithful and the catechumenate, the latter being part of the Rite of Christian Initiation of Adults (RCIA). The Prayer of the Faithful, also called the General Intercessions, follows a standard format. The priest invites the congregation to pray. A lector, deacon, or cantor then reads (or sings) the specific petitions. We make these petitions our own either by silent prayer or by a response said together after each petition, such as "Lord, have mercy" or "Lord, hear our prayer." Finally, the priest sums up all the intentions in a concluding prayer.

As a rule, the petitions are succinct and follow this sequence: for the needs of the Church (for example, Christian unity, vocations, evangelization), for civil authorities and the whole world (for example, social justice, peace among nations), for those in need (for example, the sick, the poor, the unborn, the persecuted), and for the local community (for example, deceased parishioners, newlywed couples, those recently received into the Church).

In some places, the petitions are followed by the Hail Mary. While all liturgical prayer is addressed to God, there is nothing wrong with asking the Blessed Virgin to pray with us, and for us, in the Prayer of the Faithful. As the mother of Christ, Mary is also the mother of all the faithful who constitute Christ's Body the Church. It is only fitting that we place our prayers and our whole lives into the hands of the premier Christian and Queen of all Saints. However, in keeping with the spirit of liturgical prayer, I would recommend that the Hail Mary not be used as the concluding prayer, since the purpose of the concluding prayer is to "collect" the petitions that were just made in communion with Mary and the whole Church, and to present them to the Father through Christ in the Spirit (cf. Eph 2:18).

When we pray the Prayer of the Faithful, we heed Saint Paul's admonition to pray for everyone, especially "for kings and all who are in high positions, that we may lead a quiet and peaceable life, godly and respectful in every way" (1 Tim 2:1-2). With this collection of prayers for the needs of the Church and the whole world, the Liturgy of the Word comes to an end.

The Liturgy of the Eucharist

The Preparation of the Gifts (Offertory)

Now we shift our focus from the ambo to the altar, where Christ's perfect sacrifice to the Father is made present to us under signs of bread and wine.

The Liturgy of the Eucharist begins with the Preparation of the Gifts, also called the Offertory. Originally, the faithful brought bread and wine from their homes to church to be used for the Mass and to be given to the clergy and the poor. Today we make a similar offering for the parish and the poor with our monetary contributions.

At the beginning of the rite, the deacon or a server brings the chalice to the altar. Meanwhile, ushers take up the collection as the congregation or choir sings a hymn related to the season, the feast, or the offering of the gifts. Members of the congregation come forward and present the gifts of bread and wine to the priest.

These gifts, our food and drink, represent our life; in offering them to God through the hands of the priest, we are giving God ourselves.

In the Western or Latin Church, the bread must be made of unleavened wheat and water, with no additives, thus maintaining the connection between the Eucharist and the Passover. However, the Eastern Churches (both Catholic and Orthodox) use leavened bread to symbolize both the Resurrection and the superiority of the Eucharist to the Passover (recall the line in the Holy Thursday hymn *Pange Lingua*: "O'er ancient forms departing, newer rites of grace prevail").

At the altar, the priest offers to God first the bread, then the wine. These offerings are accompanied by prayers (said silently or aloud) similar to those Jesus used at the Last Supper. Before offering the wine, the priest or deacon pours it into the chalice, adding a drop of water. In ancient times it was customary to add water because the wines were very heavy. In the Mass, the water mingled with wine has a symbolic meaning: the wine represents Christ; the water, humanity. As the priest or deacon adds the water, he prays silently: "By the mystery of this water and wine may we come to share in the divinity of Christ who humbled himself to share in our humanity."

After presenting the bread and wine, the priest bows before the altar and silently asks God to accept our gifts. Since these gifts will become Christ Himself, God will surely accept them. But since our self-offering is joined to Christ's, we must make ourselves worthy. Only by surrendering ourselves to God's will can this be done. On the paten with the bread and in the chalice with the wine, we figuratively place our hearts and our minds, our home life and our work, our joys and our sorrows: all these are offered to God in union with Christ's sacrifice.

The priest may then incense the gifts to honor them for what they are (the fruits of creation and human labor) and for what they will become (the Blessed Sacrament). If so, he then walks around the altar while incensing it (and the crucifix on or near it), after which the deacon or server honors Christ in His sacred ministers and people by incensing first the priest, then all clergy present in the sanctuary, and finally the congregation.

Next, the priest washes his hands, praying silently: "Wash me, O Lord, from my iniquity and cleanse me from my sin." This ritual symbolizes the interior purity needed to offer the Eucharist worthily. He then invites us to pray that God will accept both his sacrifice (Christ's sacramental Body and Blood) and ours (the offering of holy lives); and we respond: "May the Lord accept the sacrifice at your hands…." Finally, the priest says or sings the Prayer over the Offerings, asking God to look favorably on our oblation.

The Preparation of the Gifts finished, we are ready to enter into the heart of the Mass, the Eucharistic Prayer.

The Preface and *Sanctus*

After the presentation and offering of the gifts comes the very essence of the Holy Sacrifice: the great Eucharistic Prayer. The offerings of mere bread and wine to God are obviously inadequate. However, because they symbolize the lives of those present at Mass they become more valuable. Yet even so they are insufficient, for only that which is of infinite value is worthy of almighty God.

The real gift offered to God at Mass is our Lord Jesus Christ Himself. As was explained early on, the Mass is the sacrifice of the Body and Blood of Christ, who offers Himself on the altar, by the hands of the priest, to God, as He offered Himself on the Cross to save the world. At Mass, we are able to participate intimately in Christ's sacrifice; for the offerings on the altar, representing the offering of our lives, become Christ Himself.

The Eucharistic Prayer opens with a hymn of praise and thanksgiving called the Preface (from the Latin for "before the face," a coming before the face of God). Originally, the Preface was freely composed by the celebrant. Later it assumed a fixed format, though its content varies according to the feast or season.

The number of prefaces in the Roman Rite has varied considerably. At one time, there was virtually a preface for each Mass throughout the liturgical year; at another time, there were as few as ten. The present Roman Missal contains nearly 100 proper prefaces for Sundays and feast days, liturgical seasons, special celebrations (for example, Masses for the dead and nuptial Masses), and so on.

Each Preface has a prelude in the form of a spoken or chanted dialogue between the celebrant and the congregation. This introductory dialogue is common (with variants) to all liturgical rites of the Catholic Church and consists of simple acclamations which probably formed part of Jesus' prayer at the Last Supper:

Priest: The Lord be with you.

People: And with your spirit.

Priest: Lift up your hearts.

People: We lift them up to the Lord.

Priest: Let us give thanks to the Lord our God.

People: It is right and just.

Recall that to "give thanks" translates the Greek verb which now names the whole Mass: Eucharist.

The priest says or sings that it certainly is right and proper to thank God for all we have and are; but he is now talking to God and no longer to us. Then the text varies so as to express the theme of the particular celebration.

A startling truth is disclosed in the conclusion of the Preface: When we come before God to offer our prayer and adoration, we do so in the company of the angels and archangels and the whole company of heaven. Combining the thunderous praise of the angels as described by Isaiah (Is 6:3) with the cry of the people on Palm Sunday (Mt 21:9; cf. Ps 118:25-26), we join the celestial choirs in glorifying the Holy Trinity: *Sanctus, sanctus, sanctus…*

Holy, Holy, Holy, Holy Lord God of hosts.
Heaven and earth are full of your glory.
Hosanna in the highest.
Blessed is he who comes in the name of the Lord.
Hosanna in the highest.

The rest of the Eucharistic Prayer, or Canon, reenacts the drama of the Lord's gift of Himself. Soon Christ will become present on the altar in the sacrament of His Body and Blood, and we will stand by faith in the Upper Room and on Calvary.

The Eucharistic Prayer (Canon)

In the last chapter we looked at the Preface, which begins the Eucharistic Prayer. Now let's examine the rest of that prayer, also called the Canon, from the Greek word for "rule" or "norm" because it is the normative text according to which our gifts of bread and wine become the Body and Blood of Christ, offered to God as a sacrifice for sins and given to us as spiritual food and drink.

The modern Roman Rite features four principal Eucharistic Prayers, among which the first, the Roman Canon, holds pride of place. While these vary in style and character (as we will see later in this chapter), they are generally alike in structure.

Having given thanks for God's benefits, the priest extends his hands over the bread and wine, palms down, and in a prayer called the *Epiclesis* (Greek for "invocation") asks the Father to send the Holy Spirit to change the bread and wine into Christ's Body and Blood. In words from the Gospel texts and Saint Paul's account, he then recalls the events of the Last Supper, when Jesus offered His Body and Blood under forms of bread and wine, gave them to His apostles to eat and drink, and commanded them to do this in memory of Him (Lk 22:19; 1 Cor 11:23), that is, to offer the Eucharist as a memorial sacrifice.

Taking the bread in his hands and bowing slightly, the priest repeats Jesus' words of consecration: "THIS IS MY BODY...." God the Son, the incarnate Word, is now present on the altar. Only the "accidents" or physical properties of bread remain as they were before; but the *substance* is now Christ's Body, joined with His Blood. The priest raises the Host (from the Latin *hostia*, "victim") for all to see, replaces It on the altar and genuflects in adoration. Then, taking the chalice and bowing slightly, he says, "THIS IS THE CHALICE OF MY BLOOD...." As with the bread, the "accidents" of wine remain; but the chalice now contains Christ's Blood, joined with His Body. The priest elevates the chalice for all to see, replaces it on the altar, and genuflects. In many churches a bell is rung at each elevation, and on especially solemn occasions the deacon or server incenses the Blessed Sacrament.

Before the Consecration, the priest was speaking in the first person plural as our representative. At the Consecration, however, he uses the first person singular ("*my* Body... *my* Blood..."), for Christ is the one consecrating the Eucharist by speaking and acting through His ordained priest.

After the Consecration we say or sing a Memorial Acclamation, proclaiming (in variant forms) the Lord's death until His glorious return (1 Cor 11:26).

Now come the *Anamnesis* (Greek for "not forgetting") and Offering. In obedience to our Lord's command to remember Him, the priest recalls the saving deeds of God in Christ. But this is no mere remembrance; it is the making present again, and the recalling before God, of Christ's once-for-all sacrifice (Heb 9:25-26). The Mass gives us the opportunity of uniting our worship in a visible way with Christ's sacrifice, offering ourselves with the spotless Victim to the Father through the hands of the priest and together with him.

Because the Eucharist is celebrated in communion with the entire mystical Body of Christ, the universal Church, we remember Our Lady and the saints (the Church in heaven) and we pray for the Pope, the local bishop, and all the living and deceased faithful on pilgrimage to their heavenly home (the Church on earth and in purgatory).

Finally, our union with Christ in this sacrifice is reasserted when the priest, raising the chalice and paten (if a deacon is present, he raises the chalice) chants or says the Doxology, a hymn of praise to the Father through, with, and in Christ, in the unity of the Holy Spirit. To which we assent with a resounding "Amen."

THE FOUR EUCHARISTIC PRAYERS

We observed the general structure of the Eucharistic Prayer or Canon, the great prayer of thanksgiving, remembrance, and intercession. Incidentally, we're used to hearing the priest pray the canon aloud, but that was not always the case. From the seventh century (or perhaps earlier) until the late-1960s, the priest said most of the canon inaudibly while the people either followed along in their "hand missals" or else said other prayers of their own. Now the canon is routinely said aloud and may even be sung in its entirety. The current Roman Missal features ten canons, each having its unique style and appeal. Let's consider the first four, since these are used most frequently.

Eucharistic Prayer I is called the Roman Canon because it originated in Rome at the end of the fourth century and came into its present form during the pontificate of Saint Gregory the Great (590-604). For many centuries, this was the only canon used in the Western Church (the other three were introduced in 1968). It remained untouched until 1962, when Blessed John XXIII added Saint Joseph's name to the first of the two lists of saints mentioned. A masterpiece of theological depth and literary excellence (in its original Latin, that is), the Roman Canon consists of fifteen prayers, which can be thought of as tiles in a splendid mosaic; some of these have variants for certain occasions.

Eucharistic Prayer II is the shortest and most ancient. It is substantially the canon used in the ordination Mass of a bishop, as recorded in the *Apostolic Tradition* historically attributed to Saint Hippolytus, a Roman priest martyred in 235. The *Sanctus* ("Holy, Holy, Holy…") was added to it and its consecration narrative was edited to match that of the Roman Canon. Although it has its own preface, other prefaces may be used instead.

Eucharistic Prayer III is a completely modern composition with connections to the Gallican (old French) and Mozarabic (old Spanish) rites. It highlights the link between the Eucharistic sacrifice and the Holy Spirit who gathers us in worship, transforms bread and wine into Christ's Body and Blood, and joins together into one body those who share in the sacrificial meal of Holy Communion.

Eucharistic Prayer IV is also modern, though patterned after the Eastern rites. It gives a detailed and richly biblical account of salvation history. Like Eucharistic Prayer II, this canon has its own preface; but since this preface permits no substitutes, the Fourth Eucharistic Prayer is not used in Masses having their own special prefaces (for example, feast-days and the days of Advent and Lent).

Each canon expresses the truth that the Mass is not merely a conglomeration of prayers or a Communion service, but the most holy and sublime act of which a human being is capable: the offering of God to God! We join Jesus, the divine Son incarnate and our great High Priest, in offering His Body and Blood—sacrificed on Calvary, glorified in heaven, and sacramentally present after the consecration—to our heavenly Father for the salvation of the living and the dead:

"... we, your servants and your holy people, offer to your glorious majesty from the gifts that you have given us, this pure victim, this holy victim, this spotless victim" (EP I)

"... we offer you, Lord, the Bread of life and the Chalice of salvation" (EP II)

"... we offer you in thanksgiving this holy and living sacrifice" (EP III)

"... we offer you his Body and Blood, the sacrifice acceptable to you which brings salvation to the whole world" (EP IV)

By uniting our worship with the Savior's sacrifice, we are prepared to partake of the fruits of that offering, especially Communion, with all that this implies for our personal destiny and our relation to the whole Church.

The Communion Rite

After the Eucharistic Prayer, the Liturgy of the Eucharist continues with the Communion Rite, which we'll study in detail in this chapter. The rite begins with the Lord's Prayer or "Our Father," which Jesus taught His disciples when they asked Him to teach them how to pray (Mt 6:9-13; Lk 11:2-4). Together the priest and people sing or say this great prayer. Our baptism enables us to call God "our Father" because it has made us brothers and sisters of Christ and so children of God, to share, like any children, in the infinite wealth of our divine inheritance (see Rom 8:17). In this prayer we ask from God the best things, not only for ourselves but also for others. Because no other prayer says so much in so few words, the early Christian apologist

Tertullian (died ca. 220) described the Lord's Prayer as "truly the summary of the whole gospel."[12]

The prayer that follows is called the *Embolism*, from the Greek word for "insertion." Sung or said by the priest alone, it enlarges on the last petition of the Lord's Prayer: "... deliver us from evil." Satan, the Evil One, is the prince of this world (Jn 12:31) who builds up his dominion through the forces of pride, arrogance, and hatred. True peace, the peace of Christ, involves detachment from the evil of sin. The Embolism ends with a doxology (literally, words of praise), said or sung by the congregation, taking up the first three petitions of the Lord's Prayer: "For the kingdom, the power and the glory are yours, now and forever."

The next part of the Communion Rite is the Rite of Peace. Having recalled the risen Lord's conferral of *shalom* (Hebrew for "peace") on His apostles (Jn 20:19), the priest asks our Savior to "... look not on our sins, but on the faith of your Church..." While liturgical prayer is primarily directed to the Father, here we address the Son, asking Him to overlook our individual sinfulness and instead to regard the sinlessness of His Church. The Church as a whole is sinless because she is the Bride and mystical Body of the sinless Christ (Col 1:18; Eph 5:27; Rev 22:17) whose premier member is the sinless Virgin Mary, joined by all the saints in glory who sustain us in faith.

---

[12] Tertullian, *On Prayer* 1; quoted in the *Catechism of the Catholic Church*, no. 2761.

Now addressing the congregation, the priest wishes us Christ's peace; we answer, "And with your spirit." At the priest's discretion, he or the deacon may then invite us to exchange a sign of peace with those near us. Culture and custom determine what an appropriate gesture is. The sign of peace, said Saint Cyril of Jerusalem (315-86), signifies that "our souls are mingled together, and banish all remembrance of wrongs."[13]

We then sing or recite the *Agnus Dei* (Latin for "Lamb of God"), a prayer to Jesus recalling His announcement by Saint John the Baptist at the river Jordan (Jn 1:29). In the prophecies of the Old Testament the coming Messiah is often referred to as a lamb, the animal of choice for sacrifice. Meanwhile the priest breaks the Host in two halves in a gesture called the *fractio panis*, Latin for the "breaking of the bread," one of the earliest names for the Mass. In Jesus' day the Jews made their bread in large flat cakes. The custom then was for the head of the household to break the bread into smaller portions to be shared with those at table as a sign of unity. Jesus did just that at the Last Supper (Mt 26:26; Mk 14:22; Lk 22:19; 1 Cor 11:24). After His Resurrection it was in the breaking of the bread that His disciples recognized Him (Lk 24:35).

---

[13] Cyril of Jerusalem, *Catechetical Lectures* 23, 3; in *Nicene and Post-Nicene Fathers, Second Series,* vol. 7, *S. Cyril of Jerusalem, S. Gregory of Nazianzen,* ed. Philip Schaff and Henry Wace (New York: Christian Literature Publishers, 1894; repr. Peabody, Mass.: Hendrickson Publishers, 1995), p. 153.

As the people sing the *Agnus Dei* ("Lamb of God"), the priest drops a particle of the consecrated Host into the chalice, symbolizing the reuniting of Christ's Body and Blood at His Resurrection. He prays inaudibly: "May this mingling of the Body and Blood of our Lord Jesus Christ bring eternal life to us who receive it." In the early Church, when a bishop celebrated Mass, he broke off a fragment of the Host he had just consecrated and sent it to his priests as a sign of communion between them; when they in turn celebrated Mass, they deposited the fragment in their chalice.

Next, the priest chooses one of two short prayers said quietly as his private preparation for Communion. He genuflects, raises the Host aloft, and echoes the Baptist's cry in John 1:29: Behold, the Lamb of God! He invites us to receive Jesus, the Lamb slain for our offenses, in Holy Communion. But first we admit our unworthiness, in imitation of the centurion who asked Jesus to heal his servant (Mt 8:8). The priest consumes the Host, the Body of Christ under the appearance or "form" of bread, then the consecrated wine, Christ's Blood, saying quietly before each action: "May the Body (Blood) of Christ keep me safe for eternal life." The deacon, if present, receives Communion under both forms from the priest and may then assist the priest in administering Communion to the people.

In the Western or Latin Church, Communion has been received in various ways. The Host was received either directly on the tongue or in the hand until about the ninth century (women had to cover their hand with a white cloth), when the practice of receiving the Sacrament in the hand substantially ceased. Between the eleventh and sixteenth centuries kneeling gradually replaced standing as the communicant's posture. Communion was generally received under both forms, bread and wine, until practical and disciplinary reasons prompted the gradual withdrawing of the chalice from the laity beginning about the twelfth century. The Church teaches that in receiving either form we are receiving the whole Christ: Body, Blood, Soul and Divinity. Since Vatican II, these earlier customs have been restored as options where permitted by the local bishop.

Each country's conference of bishops determines the posture for the reception of Communion and the act of reverence to be made by each person as he or she receives it.[14] When offering us the Sacrament, the priest or other minister says, "The Body of Christ" (or "The Blood of Christ"); we answer "Amen," an act of faith that it is so.

---

[14] The bishops of the United States have decided that Communion should be received standing and that the communicant should bow before receiving; however, those who kneel or genuflect are not to be denied Communion. See U.S. Conference of Catholic Bishops, "Adaptations of the *Institutio Generalis Missalis Romani, editio typica tertia*, for the Dioceses of the United States of America," dated 14 November 2001 and available on the Internet at www.usccb.org; these adaptations were approved by the Holy See on 17 April 2002. Cf. Congregation for Divine

While Communion is distributed, the Communion Antiphon is sung. Originally a psalm with an antiphon before and after it, it is now usually a Bible verse alluding to the occasion of the Mass. A suitable hymn may be sung in place of, or in addition to, the prescribed Communion chant. If no singing occurs, the priest or people may recite the Communion Antiphon just after the priest's Communion.

After Communion, any remaining Hosts are put into the tabernacle and any remaining Precious Blood consumed. Then the priest extends the chalice to the server, who pours water into it to wash any remnants of the Sacrament. Meanwhile the priest prays silently, "What has passed our lips as food, O Lord, may we possess in purity of heart, that what has been given to us in time may be our healing for eternity." Having drunk, he dries the inside of the cup. The "purification" of the chalice and other vessels may instead be carried out by the deacon or an instituted acolyte.

The Communion Rite concludes with a period of silent thanksgiving followed by the Prayer after Communion. Standing at the altar or at his chair, the priest prays that the graces of the Sacrament remain in us as a daily help toward our salvation. With our great "Amen," the second major part of the Mass, the Liturgy of the Eucharist, is ended.

Worship and the Discipline of the Sacraments, Instruction *Redemptionis Sacramentum*, 25 March 2004, nos. 90-91.

THE CONCLUDING RITES

When the Liturgy of the Eucharist is over our tour of the Mass soon comes to an end. From what we have seen, it should be obvious why the Mass is the heart and soul of Catholicism: Christ, our crucified and risen Savior, the eternal Word and Son of the Father, descends to our altars to renew the sacrifice by which He redeemed mankind and to give Himself as the Bread of Life and pledge of resurrection (cf. Jn 6:35, 54) to those who devoutly "take and eat."

The final part of the Mass, the Concluding Rites, is also the shortest. It consists of a blessing and dismissal. Immediately following the Prayer after Communion, there may be announcements to remind us of important activities coming up in the parish. Then, for the last time, the priest greets us while standing at the altar or at his chair: "The Lord be with you." We respond: "And with your spirit." Tracing the Sign of the Cross with his right hand, he gives the blessing: "May almighty God bless you: the Father, and the Son, and the Holy Spirit." Meanwhile we bless ourselves with the Sign of the Cross and answer, "Amen."

At a bishop's Mass and on certain other occasions the form of blessing is longer and more solemn. Sometimes the blessing is preceded by a "Prayer over the People," so called because the priest extends his hands over the people while he sings or says it. The solemn blessings and prayers over the people relate to the particular theme of the liturgical season or day. When these are used, the deacon or priest first instructs us to bow our heads and pray for God's blessing.

After the blessing, the deacon (or priest, if no deacon assists) sings or says the dismissal: "Go forth, the Mass is ended" (or similar words). We answer: "Thanks be to God," a joyous acclamation for the graces received at Mass. During the Octave of Easter and again on Pentecost Sunday a double *Alleluia* follows both the dismissal and our response.

As at the beginning of Mass but in reverse order, the priest kisses the altar (as does the assisting deacon, if present), then genuflects to the Blessed Sacrament in the tabernacle (if the tabernacle is in the sanctuary) or else bows to the altar. The other liturgical ministers likewise genuflect or bow, and all exit the sanctuary. The Mass is over.

Yet in another sense the Mass never ends.

You may recall from the Introduction that the Latin words of the dismissal, "Ite, missa est," give the Eucharistic sacrifice its name. "Mass," from *missa*, means a sending forth, as on a mission. And what are we sent forth to do? It is none other than to be the embodiment of Jesus Christ in the world. This is made possible through our baptismal union with Him. This is what our communion with Him in the Holy Eucharist nourishes and increases.

The world cannot redeem itself from all that is evil, enslaving, dehumanizing, and tragic. Only sacrificial love can do that—first Christ's, then ours as members of His mystical Body. That is the essence of the Mass and so of the whole Christian life. If our worship is to mean anything, as the biblical prophets never tired of saying, it must be translated into daily mercy and justice. When our self-offering joined to Christ's is sincere, the altar becomes the platform of our charity. As we leave church, we carry Christ and His transforming love into our homes, schools, work-places, and public squares. By *loving* and *living* the Mass, we draw our earthly city closer to the heavenly City, wherein all truth, goodness, and beauty coalesce in the God whose very essence is love.

A Prayer To *Live* The Mass
by Archbishop Fulton J. Sheen

Think of how much suffering there is in hospitals, among the poor, and the bereaved. Think also of how much of that suffering goes to waste! How many of those lonesome, suffering, abandoned, crucified souls are saying with our Lord at the moment of consecration, "This is my body. Take it"? And yet that is what we all should be saying at that second:

I give myself to God. Here is my body. Take it. Here is my blood. Take it. Here is my soul, my will, my energy, my strength, my property, my wealth— all that I have. It is Yours. Take it! Consecrate it! Offer it! Offer it with Thyself to the heavenly Father in order that He, looking down on this great Sacrifice, may see only Thee, His beloved Son, in Whom He is well pleased. Transmute the poor bread of my life into Thy Divine Life; thrill the wine of my wasted life into Thy Divine Spirit; unite my broken heart with Thy Heart; change my cross into a crucifix. Let not my abandonment and my sorrow and my bereavement go to waste. Gather up the fragments, and as the drop of water is absorbed by the wine at the Offertory of the Mass, let my life be absorbed in Thine; let my little cross be entwined with Thy great Cross so that I may purchase the joys of everlasting happiness in union with Thee.

Consecrate these trials of my life which would go unrewarded unless united with Thee; transubstantiate me so that like bread which is now Thy Body, and wine which is now Thy Blood, I too may be wholly Thine. I care not if the species remain, or that, like the bread and the wine I seem to all earthly eyes the same as before. My station in life, my routine duties, my work, my family—all these are but the species of my life which may remain unchanged; but the substance of my life, my soul, my mind, my will, my heart—transubstantiate them, transform them wholly into Thy service, so that through me all may know how sweet is the love of Christ. Amen.

— From *Calvary and the Mass*

Appendix

Why a New English Translation of the Mass?

Watching a movie based on a novel you have read and enjoyed is always risky. Even though you might appreciate the film on its own merits, it is usually disappointing, even annoying, when the original story is not faithfully adapted for the screen. Of course, those who have not read the book are blissfully unaware of the discrepancies. Something similar can be said of the liturgical experience of Latin-rite Catholics over the past four decades.

When one speaks of Latin-rite Catholics today, the term does not mean that their liturgy is necessarily celebrated in Latin. That has not been the general practice since the Second Vatican Council (1962-65), which ordered a renewal of the liturgy of the Latin or Roman Rite, including the allowance for the vernacular languages to complement the traditional Latin. However much or little exposure

one has had to the original Latin words of the new
Order of Mass introduced by Pope Paul VI in 1969,
one can appreciate the vernacular liturgy for what it
is and draw spiritual nourishment from it. Those,
however, who are familiar with the authoritative
Latin text realize that a good deal has been lost in
translation. That is, until now.

In 2010, the Vatican's Congregation for Divine
Worship and the Discipline of the Sacraments gave
final approval for a new English translation of the
Mass, which replaces the one in use since 1973. The
Catholic bishops of the United States decreed that
this new translation should take effect on the First
Sunday of Advent, 2011. Many of the prayers and
responses have been reworded. The biggest changes
involve the parts said or sung by the priest.

But why, after so many years of celebrating Mass
in English, did the Church deem it necessary to have
a new translation? When the *Missale Romanum* (Roman
Missal), the book containing the official Latin words
of the Mass, was first translated into modern languages
for liturgical use, translators adopted "dynamic equivalency" as their approach to the texts.[1] This method
of translation conveys the general meaning of the

---

[1] This principle of translation was endorsed by the 1969
Instruction *Comme le prévoit*, issued by the *Consilium*, the group
charged by Pope Paul VI with implementing the liturgical reforms
outlined in the Second Vatican Council's *Constitution on the Sacred
Liturgy* (1963).

original text rather than giving a word-for-word translation. The translators sought to render the Latin words and phrases in terms immediately accessible and intelligible to all. They broke up lengthy sentences into short ones. They often chose the same English word for different Latin originals. They eliminated intensifying expressions, such as the use of multiple adjectives to modify the same noun. Dynamic equivalency made the language of prayer more simple and direct, but it did so at a high price.[2]

To begin with, there was the loss of a sacred vocabulary distinguishing the way we speak to God from the way we casually speak to other human beings. In contrast to the rhetorical humility of the Latin, the tone of the 1973 translation is at times too familiar, even chummy. So, for example, *Respicere digneris*, which literally means, "Deign to look upon," is replaced by the bald imperative, "Look." At a time when Western society is bereft of a sense of the sacred, it seemed all the more urgent to reclaim a deferential tone when addressing the all-holy God who is fearsome even as He establishes us, beyond all fear, in His love.

---

[2] In what follows, only a few examples are possible. For fuller treatments, see: Edward Sri, *A Guide to the New Translation of the Mass* (West Chester, Pa.: Ascension Press, 2011); Paul Turner, *Understanding the Revised Mass Texts*, 2nd ed. (Chicago: Liturgy Training Publications, 2010); Peter J. Elliott, "Liturgical Language: A Question of Truth," *Antiphon* 10:3 (2006) 228-38, available on the Internet at www.liturgysociety.org.

The failure of the previous translation to convey the literal meaning of the Latin is evident not only in its overall tone but also in its content. That is no small problem, since the Church prays as she believes and believes as she prays.[3] With few exceptions, the 1973 version garbles, dilutes, or actually evacuates the theological content of the original. The emphasis in many of the Latin prayers on the primacy of God's grace and our absolute dependence on it for salvation was replaced by a vague petition for help in case we falter—as if the service of God in will and in action that is necessary to win heaven were not itself the fruit of God's gift.[4] To give another example, professing Christ as "one in Being with" the Father says only that the Son exists in some relation to God, not that He is divine by reason of His being "consubstantial," or one in essence, with the Father (and the Holy Spirit). The theological accuracy of the new translation strengthens the bond between faith and worship.

Another casualty of dynamic equivalency was the link between the words of liturgy and the words of Scripture. The 1973 translation left out many of the

---

[3] As the Latin adage puts it: *Lex orandi, lex credendi* ("The law of prayer, the law of belief"), which one could paraphrase as "what you pray, you believe" (and vice versa).

[4] See Eamon Duffy, "Rewriting the Liturgy: The Theological Implications of Translation," in *Beyond the Prosaic: Renewing the Liturgical Movement*, ed. Stratford Caldecott (Edinburgh: T&T Clark, 1998), pp. 97-126.

biblical references, allusions, and images imbedded in the Latin text.[5] One example of this occurred in the Communion rite with the prayer, "Lord, I am not worthy to receive you...." The new translation repeats the prayer of the humble and compassionate centurion who asked Jesus to heal his servant: "Lord, I am not worthy that you should enter under my roof..." (Mt 8:8). Bringing the scriptures into fuller relief points up the liturgy as the principal bearer of the Church's living Tradition by which God's revealed Word comes to us, even as that Word is in many ways about liturgy.[6]

After a generation of usage, the deficiencies of the 1973 text had become widely acknowledged. In 2001, the Holy See issued the Instruction *Liturgiam Authenticam*, on the use of the vernacular languages in the publication of Roman liturgical books. In place of dynamic equivalency, *Liturgiam Authenticam* ordered a revision of the first generation of translations according to the principle of "formal equivalency," that is, a close adherence to the phrasing and vocabulary of the original texts. Since the publication in 2002 of the

---

[5] On the use of Scripture in the Mass texts, see Peter M. J. Stravinskas, *The Bible and the Mass*, rev. ed. (Mount Pocono, Pa.: Newman House Press, 2000).

[6] On the interconnectedness of Scripture and liturgy, see Scott Hahn, *Letter and Spirit: From Written Text to Living Word in the Liturgy* (New York: Doubleday, 2005).

third edition of the Roman Missal,[7] translators set to work to produce new translations of the Mass of Paul VI.

The changes contained in the new English version may be unsettling at first, but with use they will come automatically to our lips. If the process of learning new prayers and responses helps us to think about what we are singing or saying; if it helps us to grow spiritually and to appreciate the inestimable gift of the Eucharist; if it helps us even a little "to worship in spirit and truth" (Jn 4:24) then it will have been well worth the effort.

---

[7] The first official or "typical" edition of the post-Vatican II *Missale Romanum* was promulgated by Pope Paul VI in 1969 and published in 1970. The second typical edition appeared in 1975. In the Jubilee Year 2000, Blessed John Paul II approved the third typical edition, which was published in 2002 and emended in 2008; this is the Latin Missal on which the new English translation is based.

Fortescue, Adrian. *The Mass: A Study of the Roman Liturgy.* London: Longmans, Green & Co., 1912. Reprint, Albany, N.Y.: Preserving Christian Publications, 1999.

General Instruction of the Roman Missal (Third Typical Edition). Washington, D.C.: United States Catholic Conference, 2003.

Jungmann, Joseph A., S.J. *The Mass of the Roman Rite: Its Origin and Development (*Missarum Sollemnia*).* Translated by Francis A. Brunner, C.Ss.R. Revised by Charles K. Riepe. London: Burns & Oates, 1959. (Abridged, one-volume version of the English translation of the two-volume *Missarum Sollemnia.*)

Lang, Jovian P., O.F.M. *Dictionary of the Liturgy.* New York: Catholic Book Publishing, 1989.

Missale Romanum. Vatican edition of 2002, emended 2008.

Stravinskas, Peter M. J. *The Bible and the Mass,* rev. ed. Mount Pocono, Pa.: Newman House Press, 2000.

FOR FURTHER STUDY

Belmonte, Charles. *Understanding the Mass*. Princeton, N.J.: Scepter Publishers, 1997.

Benedict XVI. Apostolic Exhortation *Sacramentum Caritatis*, 22 February 2007.

Catechism of the Catholic Church. 2nd ed. Vatican City: Libreria Editrice Vaticana, 1997. See especially nos. 1066-1209, 1322-1419.

Howard, Thomas. *Evangelical Is Not Enough: Worship of God in Liturgy and Sacrament*. San Francisco: Ignatius Press, 1988.

John Paul II. Encyclical Letter *Ecclesia de Eucharistia*, 17 April 2003.

Loret, Pierre, C.Ss.R. *The Story of the Mass: From the Last Supper to the Present Day*. Translated by Dorothy Marie Zimmerman, S.S.N.D. Liguori, Mo.: Liguori Publications, 1982.

Pius XII. Encyclical Letter *Mediator Dei*, 20 November 1947.

Sheen, Fulton J. *Calvary and the Mass*. New York: P. J. Kenedy & Sons, 1936.

Suarez, Federico. *The Sacrifice of the Altar*. New York: Scepter Publishers, 1990.

Van Zeller, Dom Hubert. *The Mass in Other Words: A Presentation for Beginners*. Springfield, Ill.: Templegate Publishers, 1965.

Vatican Council II. Constitution on the Sacred Liturgy, *Sacrosanctum Concilium*, 4 December 1963.

Vonier, Abbot. *A Key to the Doctrine of the Eucharist*. London: Burns & Oates, 1925. Reprint, Bethesda, Md.: Zaccheus Press, 2003.

ABOUT THE AUTHOR

Fr. Thomas Kocik, a priest of the Diocese of Fall River, Massachusetts, is a member of the Society for Catholic Liturgy and served as editor of its journal, *Antiphon*. He is the author of *Apostolic Succession in an Ecumenical Context* (Alba House, 1996), *The Reform of the Reform? A Liturgical Debate* (Ignatius Press, 2003), and several published articles, both scholarly and popular.